St. Francis de Sales

The Life Saint Andrew

St. Francis de Sales

The Life Saint Andrew

ISBN/EAN: 9783337336837

Printed in Europe, USA, Canada, Australia, Japan

Cover: Foto ©Lupo / pixelio.de

More available books at **www.hansebooks.com**

THE LIFE

OF

SAINT ANDREW.

BOSTON:
O'LOUGHLIN & McLAUGHLIN,
630 WASHINGTON STREET.
1883.

Nothing can be more conducive to the spiritual welfare of the Faithful than to meditate on the virtues, and to consider the example, of the Saints, the chosen friends and servants of Jesus Christ. Hence, we are happy to learn that a zealous Catholic publisher has undertaken to publish a cheap edition of Lives of Saints, and we beg to recommend this work to the perusal of all faithful Christians.

✠ PAUL CULLEN,
Archbishop, etc.

THE LIFE OF SAINT ANDREW.

ST. ANDREW was born in Bethsaida, a small town of Galilee. His father was Jonas, or John, by trade a fisherman; consequently he was St. Peter's brother. He had a house in Capharnaum, and the Saviour dwelt with him whilst he was preaching in that town.

St. John Baptist having begun to preach in the desert, Andrew hastened with a burning zeal to hear his instructions, and desired to become his disciple, without engaging, however, to remain with him always. One day, hearing some one say to the holy Precursor that Jesus Christ, who was then coming out of the desert, where he had been fasting and praying for forty days, was the Lamb of God, and his faith being enlightened as to the meaning of these mysterious words, he followed the divine Saviour, with another disciple of St. John, who is not mentioned in the Gospel. They hastened with holy ardor to where Jesus was, and there they stayed with him that day and night. Oh! who can tell what effect was produced in Andrew's heart by the instructions of Jesus? He acknowledged him to be the Messiah, the Redeemer of the world, and attached himself to him for evermore. He was his first disciple.

Andrew, on his return, met Peter, and revealed to him the joy with which his heart was overflowing. "We have found,' he exclaimed, "the Messiah, the Christ promised by the prophets." Peter, thereon, would see the Christ and speak to him, and Andrew led him to the place where he had found him. Nevertheless, the two brothers did not attach themselves as yet wholly to the Saviour; they contented themselves with going to him frequently, and then returned to their calling of fishermen. Thus frequently in his society, they had ample opportunities of witnessing his wisdom, and profiting by his lessons. They were with him at the marriage in Cana, and there saw him change the water into wine. They accompanied him on the journey that he made to Jerusalem to celebrate the Pasch. About the close of the same year, our Lord, returning from lower Galilee, met the two brothers engaged fishing. He called them to him, saying he would make them "*fishers of men.*" Thereon, urged by their faith, they abandoned their nets to devote themselves to Jesus.

THE LIFE OF ST. ANDREW.

"Thus," remarks St. Chrysostom, "the divine Saviour gave them, in their own persons, a proof of what he had promised them; for it was in their regard that he, for the first time, performed the function of *a fisher of men*, inducing them to leave the world by his word and heavenly doctrine."

In the following year, our Lord formed the college of the Apostles, and the Evangelists placed Peter and Andrew over the others. A little while afterwards the Saviour visited their house in Capharnaum, where they besought him to cure the mother-in-law of Peter, and the Lord complied with their request. Some months afterwards, Jesus Christ, being moved to compassion by the sight of five thousand people who had followed him into the desert, and who were famishing with hunger, asked how they were to be fed. Andrew, full of a lively faith, answered that there was present a young man who had five barley loaves and two fishes. He added that that was very little for such a multitude; but he never doubted the intention of Jesus to manifest his omnipotence on this occasion. He therefore witnessed the miraculous multiplication of the loaves. It was Andrew who, in his zeal to make Jesus Christ known, presented to him some Gentiles who had come from Jerusalem to have the blessing of beholding the Saviour. They had been in communication with Philip, and he obtained for them the grace they desired.

After the ascension of our Lord, and the descent of the Holy Ghost, the Apostles separated to go and preach the Gospel. Andrew went to evangelize Scythia, the kingdom of Pontus, and

THE LIFE OF ST. ANDREW.

many other countries. The most constant tradition is that he gave his life for the faith at Patras, in Achaia. It is related of the Saint that, on seeing his cross at a distance, he exclaimed, "I salute thee, O cross! consecrated by the blood of my God. I approach thee with joy; receive me in thine arms. O salutary cross! how long have I sought and desired thee! My hopes at last are crowned. May he who expired on thee to ransom me, receive me through thee!" Such are the sentiments that should animate all those who desire sincerely to belong to Jesus Christ. They have no other means of proving themselves to be his true disciples.

St. Andrew's love of the cross has caused many religious associations to select him for their model and protector. "The whole world," says Bossuet, "must adore the cross. Its empire shall have no limits;

THE LIFE OF ST. ANDREW.

it will extend its dominion to the remotest religions, to the furthest islands, and to nations as yet unknown. Oh! what a glorious sight, to see barbarians and Greeks, Scythians and Arabs, and all the peoples of the world, constituting a new kingdom, whose law shall be the Gospel, and whose standard shall be the cross. Rome herself, that mighty city, after having been so long drunk with the blood of saints and martyrs of Jesus—Rome, the mistress, shall bend her head before it. She will extend her conquests further by the cross than she ever did by her arms; and we will behold more honor given to the tomb of the poor fisherman than was ever given to the temple of her Romulus. You, ye Cæsars, shall come hither too. Jesus will shatter at his feet the majesty of your empire. Constantine, the victorious emperor, at the moment marked out by Providence, shall lift the standard of the cross above the Roman eagles. By the cross he shall vanquish tyrants; by the cross he shall give peace to the empire; by the cross he will strengthen his house; the cross shall be his only trophy, because he will fearlessly proclaim that it has given him all his victories. Thou hast triumphed, O Jesus! and thou leadest in triumph, captive and trembling, the powers of darkness behind thy cross. Thou hast subdued the world not by steel, but by the wood; for, ah! it was worthy of thee to vanquish might by weakness, and the highest by the lowliest, and a false and proud philosophy by sage and modest folly. Thus hast thou shown that nothing is weak in thy hands, and that thou makest thunderbolts out of whatsoever thou willest to employ."

THE LIFE OF ST. ANDREW.

PRAYER.

St. Andrew, generous friend of the cross of our Lord, thou who hast embraced it with so much ardor, and who, after the example of thy divine Master, has bedewed it with thy blood; obtain for us by thy prayers, that like thee we may love the cross, the instrument of our salvation, and carry it as our Lord commands in the Gospel, till at length, borne upon it ourselves, we may arrive without peril in eternal beatitude.

Holy Ghost College
SCHOLASTICATE
Pittsburgh, Pa.

THE LIFE OF SAINT PETER.

PETER, son of Jona, and brother of St. Andrew, was born at Bethsaida, a town of Galilee, and was called Simon. He was a fisherman, and lived with his wife and his mother-in-law at Capharnaum, on the western extremity of the Lake of Genezareth. Andrew having heard St. John the Baptist (of whom he was a disciple) declare that Jesus Christ was the Messiah promised by the prophets, wished to see him and hear him. He accordingly went, and brought with him St. Peter, to whom our Lord immediately addressed these words: "Thou art Simon, son of Jona: thou shalt be called Cephas"; that is to say, Peter. A great mystery lay hidden beneath these words, as we shall see hereafter.

St. Peter did not attach himself to Jesus Christ at this first interview; but he visited him from time to time, and then returned to his ordinary avocations. It was chiefly owing to a second vocation that he became more particularly a disciple of Jesus Christ. One day while our Lord was walking on the bank of the Lake of Tiberias, he saw two boats, the owners of which were on the strand washing their nets. Being completely surrounded by the crowd that followed him, he went into one of the vessels which belonged to Simon, and then, putting off a short distance from the shore, he sat down and commenced preaching to the multitude.

After finishing his discourse, he said to Peter, "Launch out into the deep water and cast thy nets." Simon Peter obeyed, and instantly the two boats were so filled with fish that they were nigh being sunk. Astonished by this miracle, the son of Jona could not repress the transports of his faith and gratitude: "Lord," he exclaimed, casting himself at the feet of Jesus, "I am a sinful man; depart from me." James and John, the sons of Zebedee, his companions, were equally enraptured at sight of this miracle. Jesus, who knew their inmost thoughts, then said to them: "Follow me: hitherto you have been fishermen; but I will make ye fishers of men." Thenceforth these men of simple and upright heart quitted their nets and followed him.

Nor was it long till Peter's faith met its reward. The Redeemer condescended to visit his house, where he found his mother-in-law lying sick of fever. He who rules as supreme Lord over all things touched the hand of the infirm woman; and lo! the fever vanished!

Clement of Alexandria tells us that St. Peter was baptized by the Lord himself, and that he was the only one who received this signal favor. He likewise tells us that it was St. Peter who baptized Andrew, James, and John.

From the day on which St. Peter was called to the apostolate, he became intimately associated with his divine Master, and never left him. He, therefore, witnessed all the miracles by which he proved his heavenly mission. But we will cite only those in which the Evangelists mention his presence.

Having wrought the great miracle of the multiplication of the loaves, and after having dismissed the multitude, who, to attest their gratitude, would have carried him off and proclaimed him their king, Jesus ordered his disciples to go into a boat, while he retired alone to a mountain to pray. Suddenly a tempest sprang up and the fragile bark with its crew was on the point of being whelmed in the raging waters; but, lo! at the fourth watch of the night Jesus Christ walks towards them on the waves. The apparition appalled them, and, mistaking him for a phantom, they uttered a cry of horror: "Be of good heart," said Jesus to them, "'tis I." And Peter, making answer, said: "Lord, if it be thou, bid me come to thee upon the waters." And he said, "Come"; and Peter, going down out of the boat, walked upon the water to come to Jesus; but seeing the wind strong he was afraid; and, when he began to sink, he cried out, saying, "Lord, save me." And immediately Jesus, stretching

forth his hand, took hold of him, and
said, "O thou of little faith, why dost
thou doubt?" They both then entered
the boat, and the tempest ceased. All
those who were present, seeing this
miracle, approached Jesus, and adored
him, saying, "Thou art truly the Son
of God." Peter, certainly, was not the
last to confess the divinity of him who
commanded the winds and waves; but a
moment was approaching in which he
was to confess him still more openly.

Jesus Christ had now come to the
neighborhood of Cæsarea Philippi, the
last town of Judea on the north, situated
at the foot of Mount Hermon, a portion
of the chain of Lebanon. Here, in one
of those familiar interviews in which he
took occasion to instruct his disciples, he
put this question to them: "Whom do
men say that I am?" "Lord," they an

swered, "some say that thou art John Baptist; others that thou art Elias; and others that thou art Jeremias, or some one of the prophets." "And you," resumed Jesus, "whom do you say that I am?" "Lord," replied Peter, speaking in the name of all the disciples, "thou art Christ, the Son of the living God." "Blessed art thou, Simon Bar-Jona"—thus spake Jesus to him—"for 'tis not flesh and blood that hath revealed this to thee, but my Father who is in heaven." And then, to recompense the ardent faith of the prince of the apostles, he added: "And I tell thee that thou art Peter, and that on this rock I will build my church, against which the powers of hell shall never prevail."

On this memorable day in which the primacy of St. Peter was so evidently established, this was not the only favor bestowed on him by his divine Master.

Having now been constituted the fundamental stone of the terrestrial church, he was appointed to lead the faithful into the heavenly city, for Jesus Christ bestowed on him the keys of the kingdom of heaven—in other words, the power of loosing and binding. In a word, he gave to him, as well as to the other apostles, the power of remitting or retaining sins in confession, and this power was to be transmitted through them to their successors.

Meanwhile the time was nigh at hand in which the Saviour was to consummate, on Calvary, the work of our redemption. Desiring to prepare his apostles for this terrible scene, he began by revealing to them that he must go to Jerusalem, where he was to suffer much at the hands of senators, scribes, and priests; in a word, that he was to be put to death, and that he would arise three days afterwards.

Peter, listening only to his love for his divine Master, began, according to the expression of the Evangelist, to "rebuke him," saying, "Lord, that shall never happen unto thee." On hearing this, Jesus blamed him severely, and reproached him for having taste only for the things of earth.

Peter's fault was truly a pardonable one, for it sprang from love. Six days afterwards, says the Evangelist, Jesus took with him Peter, James, and John his brother, and conducted them up to a high mountain, which is commonly believed to be Thabor. There he was transfigured before them; his countenance became brilliant as the sun, and his garments as white as snow. At the same time Moses and Elias appeared and conversed with him. On witnessing such a glorious spectacle, Peter could not contain his admiration and joy. "Lord," he exclaimed, "it is well for us to be here; let us make three tabernacles, one for you, one for Moses, and one for Elias."

Whilst Peter was still speaking, a luminous cloud enveloped Jesus, Moses, and Elias, and then was heard a loud voice saying, "This is my dearly beloved Son, hear ye him." At sight of those transcendent wonders, the apostles were overwhelmed with a sort of stupor, and they all three fell with faces prostrated on the ground. Jesus then approached them, and touching them with his hand, said, "Arise, fear nothing." They looked about them; Moses and Elias had disappeared. The first, the author of the written law; and the second, representing the prophets, or rather the law and the prophets, in their persons, had come solely to render homage to the superiority of the new law.

Their ministry was accomplished; and now no one was to be heard save the Son of God alone.

The Pasch, the greatest of all the Jewish festivities, had now arrived. The object of this festival was to symbolize everything that had reference to the sacrifice of the new law and the mystery of the world's redemption. When night had come, says the sacred text, Jesus sat at table with his twelve disciples to celebrate the Pasch, the last that was to be celebrated according to the rite instituted by Moses, and the first in which the true Paschal Lamb was to replace that which was merely its figure. Towards the close of the repast, Jesus laid aside his garment, and girded himself with a towel; then, having poured water into a basin, he washed the feet of his disciples, and dried them with the towel wherewith he was girded.

Astounding as was this act of humility, the Evangelist does not say that any of the disciples except St. Peter resisted it. When it came to his turn to have his feet washed, he thus evinced his surprise: " Lord, thou shalt never wash my feet!" " If I do not wash thy feet," replied Jesus, " thou shalt not have part with me." " Lord," rejoined St. Peter, with all the ingenuousness of a happy soul, " on that condition wash not only my feet, but my hands and head likewise."

Jesus Christ had forewarned his disciples that one of them was about to betray him. The very thought of this filled him with sorrow, and he then bade them adieu tenderly, and exhorted them to love each other affectionately, as he himself had loved them. All the disciples of the Lord wept while listening to these words, and Simon Peter in particular was deeply affected by them. "Lord," he asked, "whither goest thou?" Jesus answered, "I am going where thou canst not follow me now." "Why, Lord, may I not follow thee now? if necessary, I will lay down my life for thee." "Amen, I say to thee," was our Lord's answer, "before the cock crows twice, thou shalt have three times denied me." There is in this something calculated to confound us. This man of zeal, this apostle whose faith we have seen manifesting itself so gloriously—this apostle is going to deny his Master. Ah! beneath this appearance of entire devotion to his sacred person, the eye of Jesus Christ detected some lingering trace of presumption and self-love which must have its chastisement. But the repentance and bitter grief that this fall brings to the soul of St. Peter will teach him to cherish condescension and all necessary charity for his brethren.

We find St. Peter in the Garden of Olives. He accompanied Jesus with the two sons of Zebedee, when the Lord retired to this place, with soul sickened unto death. When Judas came to give the Redeemer the traitor's kiss—the preconcerted signal by which his enemies were to identify him—Peter, in the ardor of his zeal, unsheathed a sword, and cut off the ear of the servant of the high-priest. Doubtless he would have killed him, had not Jesus interposed. At this direful crisis, all the other disciples fled away in terror. Peter, however, clung to his Lord, and followed him to the residence of Caiphas. Here he sat down in the vestibule with the servants of the high-priest, waiting the issue of this great business, and following all its sad details with painfully anxious interest. During these hours of agony, a servant-woman of the high-priest approached, and said, "You, too, were with Jesus of Galilee." Peter denied this, and answered, "I know not what you say." An instant afterwards, another servant, on seeing him, said to those who were about her: "He yonder was also with Jesus of Nazareth." Peter denied this still more energetically, and answered, "I swear that I do not know this man." Just then the cock crew, but Peter heard it not. A little afterwards, one of those who were there, a relative of Malchus, whose ear Peter had cut off in the Garden of Olives, advanced, and said to him, "Of a certainty you were along with them, your language betrays you." Then, as it were to put the crown on his inexcusable obstinacy, Peter pronounced horrible imprecations, and repeated with an oath that he knew not the man. Just then the cock crew a second time. Then it was that the faithless disciple encountered the divine eyes of Jesus. His glance subjugated the apostle's heart. On the moment, he beheld the depth of his fall and the magnitude of his crime. His heart was melting in his bosom, and he went out into the courtyard to give free course to his repentant tears.

This abandonment on the part of the apostles, and this denial on the part of St. Peter—the bitterest ingredients in the chalice of the Lord's sufferings—prove to us that the Lord was pleased to choose the weakest instruments for the establishment of the kingdom of the Gospel. They prove, moreover, that the establishment of Christianity is its greatest miracle.

THE LIFE OF ST. PETER.

Meanwhile, after our Lord had been overwhelmed with injuries and insults, scourged, crowned with thorns, spat upon, buffeted, and nailed to the cross on which he expired, his dead body was laid in a tomb. Nothing was left undone to make him appear an object of scandal to the eyes of his apostles; and Peter, like the others, although he had frequently heard Jesus speak of his resurrection, could think of nothing but the coming miracle that was to set the seal on all the others which had so gloriously signalized the Redeemer's life. But the third day after our Lord's death, certain pious women proceeded early in the morning to the sepulchre with perfumes that they had prepared, and great was their astonishment when they found that the stone had been rolled away from its mouth, and that the body was no longer there

THE LIFE OF ST. PETER.

In the meantime, two persons utterly unknown to them presented themselves, and recounted to them the wonders that had been operated. They then hastened to relate these things to the other apostles. Hearing this, Peter and John arose and hurried to the sepulchre. There they found nothing but the winding-sheet and some linen, which the Saviour had flung off. St. John, speaking of this, says that he thenceforth believed on the testimony of his own eyes, and he adds also, in speaking of St. Peter: "For as yet they knew not the Scripture, that he must rise again from the dead."

On the night of the same day, Peter saw the Lord himself; for, while the apostles were assembled together in a chamber whose doors were locked, on account of their fear of the Jews, Jesus appeared and said to them, "Peace be with you." He then showed them his pierced hands and opened side; and, after saying a second time, "Peace be with you," he added, "As my Father hath sent me, I also send you." He then breathed upon them, and said; "Receive the Holy Ghost; whose sins you shall forgive, they are forgiven them; and whose sins you shall retain, they are retained."

Eight days afterwards, the disciples being still assembled in the same place, Jesus appeared while the doors were locked as on the former occasion. Standing in the midst of them, he saluted them with the ordinary salutation, "Peace be with you."

Peter, moreover, with many other disciples, was blessed by another manifestation of the Lord on the borders of the lake of Tiberias. They had gone to fish, for those laborious men had not totally abandoned their toilsome occupations, since they were obliged to support themselves by the sweat of their brows. They entered a boat, and, after laboring all night, took nothing. Morning having come, Jesus appeared on the bank, without being recognized by his disciples, and said to them, "Children, have you nothing to eat?" "No," replied they. "Cast your nets on the right of the boat," said the Lord. They did so, and they could not drag in the net, so heavily was it laden with fishes.

John, seeing this, said to Peter, "It is the Lord!" The mention of his name was enough for Peter. He put on his clothes, for he was naked, and cast himself into the water to go and meet his divine Master, while the other disciples followed in a boat. They all sat down to eat on the bank of the lake. **After** the repast, Jesus said to Peter, " Simon, lovest thou me more than those ?" " Lord," replied the apostle, " thou knowest I love thee."—" Feed my lambs," said Jesus. Jesus asked him a second time, " Simon, lovest thou me more than those ?" " Yes," answered Peter, " I love thee, and thou knowest it."—" Feed my lambs."

A third time did the Redeemer put the same question to Peter. A profound sadness had now seized the apostle, and he answered, " Lord, thou knowest all things—thou knowest that I love thee." Then Jesus said to him, " Feed my sheep." By these words he gave him power not only over the mere faithful, but also over the pastors themselves. " Amen, amen, I say to thee, when thou wast young, thou didst gird thyself, and didst walk where thou wouldst; **but** when thou shalt be old, thou shalt stretch forth thy hands, and another shall gird thee, and lead thee whither thou wouldst not. And this he said, signifying by what death he should glorify God."

Jesus Christ appeared once more, for the last time, to his disciples, before ascending into heaven. It was then that he most signally gave them their apostolic mission—"Go through the whole world . . . preach the Gospel to every creature . . . and believe firmly that I will be with you even to the consummation of ages. I am going to send you the gift of my Father that has been promised to you. Remain in the city; do not quit Jerusalem till you are clothed with strength from on high." Then, having gone with them to the Mount of Olives, he blessed them for the last time, and ascended into heaven.

THE LIFE OF ST. PETER.

The apostles returned to Jerusalem, under the guidance of Peter, to await the coming of the Holy Ghost.

As soon as the apostles were filled with the Holy Ghost, they began to speak in various languages. The incredulous, who scoff at everything, said that they were drunken men. Peter then, to meet their incredulity, showed clearly that this fact was merely the fulfilment of prophecy; and his words converted three thousand persons, who asked baptism at his hands. A short time after this, the preaching of the prince of the apostles converted five thousand persons more.

To the power of the words that the Holy Ghost put in their mouths the apostles added the evidence of miracles, and they loudly proclaimed that it was in the name of Jesus of Nazareth that they wrought them. Their persecutors knew not how to answer them. To deny the miracles was impossible—all Jerusalem beheld them; they therefore resolved that the fame of them should not be diffused abroad through the world. They consequently forbade the apostles to mention the name of Jesus to any one. "Judge yourselves," said St. Peter to them, "whether it be just in the eyes of God to obey him rather than you. As for us, it is impossible for us not to speak of the things which we have heard and seen." Their judges, confounded by this answer, dismissed them, after threatening them with punishment. Once more at liberty, they all assembled together, and they all celebrated the power of the Lord in a hymn of thanksgiving.

Nothing could have been more admirable than the holy society they had formed. Those who possessed property in houses or lands sold it, through love of poverty and in the spirit of charity. They then brought the money to the feet of the apostles, who distributed it amongst the faithful according to their wants. One day a man named Ananias, having sold his lands, formed a plan with his wife, named Sapphira, to retain a portion of the price which he had received. He then carried the remainder of the sum to the feet of the apostles, to whom he said that he had not retained anything. It was not to man, but to God himself, that he lied, as St. Peter told him; and thus his crime could not go unpunished. He suddenly fell dead, struck by an invisible hand, and his wife, who came a few hours afterwards to sustain the lie, perished in the same manner.

The miracles of the apostles were multiplied day by day, and those of St. Peter in particular were so signal that the sick and afflicted were brought out whenever he passed, in order that his shadow might fall on them, and restore them to health Witnessing such indisputable miracles, the enemies of the apostles redoubled their fury, and cast them into prison. Vain efforts! An angel of the Lord came to deliver them. They raged; but they always received this answer: "It is better to obey God than to obey man." They were then released, and went about rejoicing that they had been deemed worthy to suffer this outrage for the name of their divine Master.

These persecutions tended only to inflame still more the zeal of the apostles, and the number of the faithful increased daily. There was among the new converts a certain Simon, who was reputed to be skilled in the pretended arts of magic.

THE LIFE OF ST. PETER.

This man, seeing that Peter and John conferred the Holy Ghost by the imposition of hands, furnished himself with a sum of money, and went to offer it to them, saying, "Bestow on me the power that you exercise, in order that those on whom I impose hands may also receive the Holy Ghost." Odious traffic! As though the gifts of the Holy Ghost were marketable for a sum of gold, like vulgar merchandise. This infamous proposition excited Peter's indignation: "Let your money perish with you," said he, "since you have believed that the gift of God could be bought with money." Simon saw his fault, and showed his sorrow; but it is doubtful if his sorrow was sincere, or at least lasting. His dishonored name serves even to this day to designate those who traffic in holy things, as does that of Judas to designate traitors. The former are termed Simonists

Peter undertook various journeys through Judea to visit the faithful, and confirm them in the faith, that is to say, for the purpose of giving them the Sacrament of Confirmation. He found at Lydda, a town of the tribe of Ephraim, a man named Eneas stretched on his bed by paralysis. "Eneas," said the apostle to him, "the Lord Jesus Christ healeth thee, arise and make thy bed"; and immediately he arose, as strong and healthy as he had before been languid and sick. The fame of this miracle was soon diffused through all the neighboring towns, and the inhabitants of Joppa sent to Peter, beseeching him to come and visit them. When he arrived, they brought him to a chamber where lay the mortal remains of a woman named Tabitha or

Dorcas, who was illustrious for her virtues and good works. They gave the apostle to understand by their tears and groans that the deceased was deserving of Heaven's mercy. Peter knelt to pray, for he was moved to pity, and as soon as he knew that God had heard him, he said, "Talitha, arise!" and she got up on the instant, to the astonishment of all around her. This miraculous cure and resurrection produced abundant fruits of conversion throughout the whole country.

Up to this moment the Jews alone seemed to have been called to the faith; but the time in which the Gentiles, that is to say, the pagans, were to become participators of it, had arrived. At Cesarea there was a centurion of Roman origin named Cornelius, who gave copious alms and devoted much time to prayer.

One day an angel appeared to him, and told him that his alms had ascended in the sight of God, who wished to recompense him. "There is at this moment in Joppa," said the angel, "a certain Simon, surnamed Peter, lodging in the house of another Peter, a currier, near the sea. Send to seek him; it is he who will teach you what you have to do." Thereon Cornelius immediately sent for St. Peter. Meanwhile, the apostle had had a vision. He beheld the heavens opened, and an immense sheet let down by the four corners descending towards the earth. On this sheet was every sort of animal. At the same time he heard a voice saying, " Peter, arise, kill and eat." "God forbid, Lord," replied he, " that I should ever eat anything common or defiled." And then the voice was heard again saying, "Peter, call not that defiled which God himself has purified." This vision appeared to him thrice, and then the great sheet was taken back into heaven.

Peter was still occupied thinking what this vision could mean, when the Spirit of God said to him, " Behold, three men are seeking thee: arise, make no difficulty about going with them: for it is I who have sent them." Peter, on meeting the messengers, immediately understood their object. He therefore proceeded to the centurion at Joppa, and besought him to hear the word of God preached to him and his household. While Peter was preaching, the Holy Ghost descended on the Gentiles who were listening to him. The apostle then said, could we refuse the water of baptism to those who have already received the Holy Ghost as well as we? He then immediately commanded them to be baptized.

Thus was the line of demarcation between the Gentiles and the people of God effaced, and thus was the faith given to all men. Some Jews there were who reproached Peter for his conduct in regard of the Gentiles. "Since God," replied the apostle, "has accorded them the same grace that he has given to us, who have believed in the Lord Jesus Christ, who am I, weak mortal, that I should oppose myself to the designs of God?" These words pacified them, and they began to glorify God, saying, "God, then, hath also to the Gentiles given repentance unto life."

It was about this period that St. Peter went to dwell at Antioch, where the faithful were, for the first time, called Christians. Scarcely had he arrived when Herod, the king, caused him to be arrested. Laden with chains, he was cast into a

THE LIFE OF ST. PETER.

dungeon, and the tyrant determined to put him to death. All the Church mourned and prayed for its chief. There was now only one night between Peter and the day of his execution. Nevertheless, the apostle had confidence in God, and he slept tranquilly amongst his guards. Suddenly a heavenly light flooded the prison. It was the liberating angel who came to announce to Peter his enfranchisement. In an instant the chains fell from his hands, the doors flew open before him, and he walked out to rejoin his brethren.

The Gospel was every day making progress and spreading over the world rapidly. But some of those who preached it, having a hankering after Judaism, pretended that one could not be saved without being circumcised according to the law of Moses. St. Paul and St. Barnabas, who were evangelizing the Gentiles, pronounced energetically against this doctrine. It was resolved, therefore, that they should meet at Jerusalem, for the deciding of this question. *Jerusalem was then the centre of unity, because Peter was there.* This was the first council. Peter, who presided, then spoke thus: " God put no difference between us and them [the Gentiles], purifying their hearts by faith. But by the grace of the Lord Jesus Christ, we believe to be saved, in like manner as they also." St. Paul, St. Barnabas, and St. James supported this grand and powerful voice of Catholicity; and it was concluded that the Gentiles who had come into the Church should not be disquieted by the question of circumcision. Never was the supremacy of St. Peter over the other apostles more clearly manifested than in this celebrated council of Jerusalem.

THE LIFE OF ST. PETER.

The apostles now portioned out the nations according to the order in which they were to be evangelized. In this grand division, St. Peter chose to preach the faith to the Jews dispersed over Pontus, Galatia, Bithynia, Cappadocia, and throughout the greater part of Asia. Whilst he was at Cesarea, Simon the magician, of whom we have already spoken, proposed to have an interview with him. When they met, Simon commenced to boast that he could perform every sort of miracle. A few words from Peter were quite sufficient to confound him on this subject: "He," said the apostle, "who derives his mission from hell works wonders that are useless to every one. Tell us, Simon, what does it avail you to set your statues in motion? What good do you achieve by flying in the air? All the miracles of Jesus were for the benefit of mankind. He gave hearing to the deaf, and sight to the blind. He healed the lame, and caused the dead to arise. Simon, dost thou comprehend the difference?"

And, in sooth, he did comprehend it, for he soon became a laughing-stock to the people he had long deceived, so much so that he was obliged to quit Cesarea, to hide the shame of his defeat. All those who had been his disciples now fell at Peter's feet, and gladly abjured their errors.

From Cesarea, St. Peter went to Tripoli, in Phenicia, then to Laodicea, and finally to Antioch. Simon had preceded him to the latter city; but the defeat sustained at Cesarea caused the people to look on him with a feeling of contempt. Peter, on the other hand, was received most enthusiastically. He wrought a great many miraculous cures; he excited the people to repent and believe in Jesus Christ, and within seven days more than ten thousand persons were baptized. Theophilus, the most distinguished of all the denizens of Antioch, gave up his house to the apostle, who converted it into a church, and the people erected the chair from which Peter daily preached to them the word of God. St. Peter was the first bishop of Antioch.

But it was the will of the Most High that he should fix his See in Rome. He knew that, as long as the great capital of the pagan world remained unconverted, Christianity must have a very precarious existence. He therefore embarked for Italy, visiting Greece and Sicily, and landed at Naples. He arrived at Rome in the second year of the reign of Claudius. He there preached the Gospel with so much success that those who heard him besought St. Mark, his disciple, to commit the Apostle's discourses to writing. In compliance with their wish, Mark wrote the Gospel that bears his name.

A short time after his arrival in Rome, Peter consecrated two bishops, Linus, who succeeded him, and Cletus or Anaclete, who succeeded Linus. The assistance of these coadjutors permitted him to absent himself from Rome, in order to go into the East. But he one day had a vision, in which he heard Jesus Christ saying, "The time of thy death approaches, and thou must return to Rome." He obeyed this order, and went back to the imperial city, where Simon the magician was now carrying on his impostures. This seducer had deluded the people so far that they were going to raise a statue to him as though he were a god. Nero, Claudius's successor, fancied that the power of this man was destined to eternize the glories and empire of Rome.

But Simon's prosperity was to be short-lived, for Peter, accompanied by Paul, recently arrived at Rome, presented himself to Nero, and reproached him for his blind credulity in believing the magician.

Nero was astonished at the boldness of the Apostle, and it is likely that his faith in Simon Magus began to be shaken. The magician trembled for his credit and glory; he therefore had recourse to audacity, and challenged Peter to meet him as on the former occasion at Cesarea, but he was defeated. Simon undertook to raise a man from the dead: he thought that he had succeeded, for the dead man moved his head, and all the spectators were enraptured. "If the dead man has really come back to life," said St. Peter, "let him get up, walk, and speak; command Simon to withdraw from the corpse, and you shall see if the person be living." Simon retired, and the body moved not. St. Peter then knelt to pray, and, lo, the dead man arose and walked!

Withal Simon did not look on himself as vanquished. He promised that he would fly through the air, and ascend to heaven to sit beside Jupiter. On the appointed day, he flew in mid-air from the hill of the Capitol, while Nero extolled his triumph, and insulted the two Apostles who were looking on. But Peter prayed aloud to God, and commanded the devils who had borne their champion through the air to abandon him; on the instant the magician tumbled to the ground, and was killed full in the sight of all the people.

The ignominious death of Simon exasperated Nero's hatred of the Christians, and particularly of the two Apostles. He caused them to be arrested, condemned to death, and cast into prison. St. Paul was beheaded, and St. Peter was crucified like his Divine Master, of whom he was the representative on earth. Peter was about eighty years of age; he was bishop of Antioch eleven years, and bishop or pope of Rome for twenty-five years, less six months and nineteen days.

The place of St. Peter's martyrdom was the Janiculum Mount at Rome, where the spot of his crucifixion is still shown. The Prince of the Apostles was crucified with his head downwards, as he did not deem himself worthy to be crucified like his Divine Master.

PRAYER.

O God! who hast glorified thy Church

THE LIFE OF ST. PETER.

by the martyrdom of thy glorious Apostle Peter, grant that we may, in all things, follow the directions of him by whom was laid the foundation of religion.

Holy Ghost College
SCHOLASTICATE,
Pittsburgh, Pa.

THE LIFE
OF
THE BLESSED VIRGIN MARY.

A Redeemer had been promised to fallen man. The Word of God himself was to become man, to redeem us, and it was in a virgin's womb that this great mystery was to be operated. The time fixed by the prophets for this work of love had now arrived.

Therefore, in the year after the creation of the world, 3985, or thereabouts, and as is generally believed, on the 8th of September, there was born in Nazareth, a small town of Galilee, this most blessed Virgin, who was destined to give birth to the Redeemer of men, the Messias whom all the ages awaited. Joachim.

her father, descended from the race of David, and Anne, her mother, sprung from the priestly family of Aaron, had miraculously obtained this child after twenty years' sterility.

This most blessed Virgin, the future mother of the Sun of Justice, was adorned with all the attributes of grace, and from the moment of her conception, no stain, even of original sin, ever tarnished her purity. Even the very day of her nativity has been inscribed amongst the number of the solemnities of the Church, while with the Saints the Church generally commemorates only the day of their death.

This child so peculiarly favored by God, received the mysterious name of Mary, which in Hebrew, signifies "STAR OF THE SEA." St. Bernard observes, that the Mother of Christ could not have received a name more suited to her destiny. "Mary," says he, "is that brilliant star which shines upon the vast and stormy sea of the world."

Twenty-four days after Mary's birth, Anne, in obedience to the law of Moses regarding purification, repaired to the Temple, and there made the usual offering, which consisted of a lamb or, from the poor, two turtle doves.

But the gratitude of Anne exceeded this; she offered to the Lord a purer victim; she devoted to the service of the holy place the infant whom the Most High had given her; and she solemnly promised to bring her child to the Temple, and there to consecrate her as soon as her young reason could discern good and evil. When the ceremony had terminated, the two spouses retraced their steps homewards; but three years had scarcely passed when the pious mother brought her daughter back. In this infant of blessedness, reason had scarcely a dawning; it beamed forth brilliantly at an age when other children scarcely know their right hand from the left. Beyond doubt, the sacrifice which these parents were about to make, cost them much. She was their only child, the sweet crown of their old age, their consolation and delight; but they were animated by the Spirit from above. Anne and Joachim preferred what was due to God to their own gratification.

Mary's father and mother, therefore, proceeded to Jerusalem, and in the midst of the imposing solemnities of the feast of the Dedication, presided over by the high priest, Zachary, deposited within the sacred precincts of the Temple the child of grace, the precious treasure that had been given to them by the God of Israel.

From that moment Mary was numbered amongst the young virgins attached to the service of the Temple, and who were brought up in the holy place, far from the noise of the world and the gaze of the wicked. An azure-colored robe, a white tunic fastened by a cincture, and a long veil, was the costume of Mary and her companions in the Temple. The virgins rose at break of day, at the hour when the *wicked angels are dumb*, says a pious author, *and when prayers are heard most favorably*. They chanted the Psalms night and morning in the sanctuary; during the day their fingers plied the cedar spindles; they worked either at gold or fine wool, and they embroidered or executed designs rivalling the fabrics of Sidon. Mary, superior to all her companions in the various pursuits, excelled them likewise in spinning. The popular traditions, faithful to this remembrance, appropriately term the white tissues of vapors suspended over the fields in the sunset of autumn, "the Virgin's threads."

Mary had passed nine years near the holy tabernacles, when she lost her aged father, who died blessing his child. A little while afterwards Anne also died. Mary, now an orphan, and bereft of all that she loved on earth, turned her thoughts undivided to the things of God. She chose God for her sole heritage, and she devoted herself to the service of his altar, with the intention of never quitting the holy place. Like the august chief of her race, Mary found that one day spent in the tabernacles of the God of Israel was preferable to a thousand days elsewhere, and she would rather have been the least in this holy place than the most honored in the tents of Cedar.

LIFE OF THE BLESSED VIRGIN MARY.

It is thus that the Blessed Virgin, who should be a model to all ages and to all the conditions of life, presents to the world, from her tenderest years, an example of that religious life which is not marked by any one distinguishing virtue, because it is an assemblage of all virtues. Above all things, Mary cultivated that virginity which Jesus Christ was to teach to the world; nay, she vowed herself to it before the Savior of the world had preached its advantages, or enunciated precepts concerning it. Before the paths had been traced, or the way opened, Mary's love served her for a master, and her heart acted as her guide. Excited and animated by grace, she was able to practise virtues till that moment unknown.

After the death of her parents, Mary was placed under guardians whose names have not reached us. In all probability they were of the sacerdotal race, since she belonged to the family of Aaron, by her mother's side. "If we be permitted to hazard a conjecture," says the Abbe Orsini, "we would say, it is likely that the charge of her education was particularly confided to the husband of Elizabeth, the high reputation of whose virtue and close kindred would seem to have marked him out for these protecting offices. The intense love that caused the Blessed Virgin, two or three years afterwards, to traverse all Judea that she might offer her congratulations to the mother of St. John the Baptist, and her protracted sojourn in the mountains of Hebron, seem to denote relations more than those of simple kindred. The roof that sheltered Mary during such a long visit could not have been, according to the usages rigorously observed by the Jews, less sacred than the paternal home."

Whosoever these guardians were, they

soon determined to give their pupil a spouse worthy of her. Mary was then, according to the common opinion, about fifteen or sixteen years of age. Cardinal Cajetan thinks that she must have been at the least twenty-two years old.

This projected marriage alarmed the young virgin. She would have resisted it; but sterility being then looked upon as a disgrace, and her vow of virginity becoming null by the sole will of the family council, Mary must needs obey. Her suitors presented themselves, and of them all the lot fell upon a poor carpenter of Nazareth, a man advanced in years (aged about fifty years), and who, although of the noble race of David, earned his bread by the sweat of his brow. An ancient tradition, given by St. Jerome, and preserved in the history of Mount Carmel, relates, that the suitors, after beseeching

Him who presides over men's destinies, deposited in the night time their almond wands in the Temple, and that on the next day the withered and dead wand of Joseph was found verdant and flourishing, like that which, in ages long gone, had secured the priesthood to the family of Aaron.

Such was the man chosen by God to be, in the eyes of men, the spouse of Mary, but in the eyes of heaven, the protector and guardian of her virginity. The humble Joseph received Mary in his poor home, and as a profound admirer of the virtues of his spouse, he respected her as the ark of the Lord, nay, as the temple of Jehovah. Mary, bidding adieu to the cedar and gold of the Temple, the consecrated perfumes, the psaltery of lyres and harps, and to all the brilliant and beauteous occupations of the holy place, clothed herself with indigence as a robe of honor, and gave herself without murmuring to all the fatiguing cares of her poor household. And why should not the pious Mary love Joseph?—by what countless cares should she not prove her gratitude to him, since her virginity, that treasure so dear to her heart, found such sure and holy protection beneath the shade of his virtues?

About two months had passed over the heads of these chaste spouses in the house of Nazareth, where they led the most holy life that heaven ever beheld, when the hour destined for the world's salvation came, that hour so often announced by the Pophets of Israel, and so long expected by the nations. Let us hear the evangelical historian: "And in the sixth month, the Angel Gabriel was sent from God into a city of Galilee, called Nazareth to a virgin espoused to a man whose name

LIFE OF THE BLESSED VIRGIN MARY.

was Joseph, of the house of David: and the virgin's name was Mary. And the angel being come in, said unto her: Hail, full of grace, the Lord is with thee: Blessed art thou among women. Who having heard was troubled at his saying, and thought with herself what manner of salutation this should be. And the angel said to her: Fear not, Mary, for thou hast found grace with God. Behold thou shalt conceive in thy womb, and shalt bring forth a son; and thou shalt call his name Jesus. He shall be great, and shall be called the son of the Most High, and the Lord God shall give unto him the throne of David his father: and he shall reign in the house of Jacob for ever."—St. Luke, i. 26–32.

Mary, not being able to comprehend these strange words, manifestly contradicting the vow of virginity she had made in the Temple of the Lord, grew more astonished. She then says to the angel, with simplicity, "How shall this be done?" And the angel answering, said to her; "The Holy Ghost shall come upon thee, and the power of the Most High shall overshadow thee. And therefore also the Holy which shall be born of thee shall be called the Son of God. And behold thy cousin Elizabeth, she also hath conceived a son in her old age; and this is the sixth month with her that is called barren; because no word shall be impossible with God."–St. Luke, i. 35–37. Mary, then annihilated before the divine decrees, replies, with the most sincere humility, "Behold the handmaid of the Lord, be it done to me according to thy word." And the angel disappeared. 'And the Word was made Flesh, and dwelt amongst us." "Let us go no further into this mystery," says St. John Chrysostom, "nor let us ask how the Holy Ghost could operate this miracle in the Virgin. This divine generation is a profound abyss that no curious searching can fathom."

Meanwhile, the Blessed Virgin being informed by the angel of the miraculous pregnancy of St. Elizabeth, believed it her duty to go and offer her congratulations. The distance between Nazareth and the town of Hebron, where dwelt the Blessed Virgin's relative, the spouse of Zachary, was about a hundred and fifteen or twenty miles; nevertheless she did not hesitate, but traversed the mountains of Judea, and at length arrived in the city of Juda. Being conducted to the house of Zachary, she entered, and saluting Elizabeth, said to her, "Peace be with thee." At the sound of Mary's voice, the precursor of the Messias leaped with joy in his mother's womb, and Elizabeth, filled with the spirit of prophecy, exclaimed, "Blessed art thou among women, and blessed is the fruit of thy womb. And whence is this to me, that the Mother of my Lord should come to me? For behold, as soon as the voice of thy salutation sounded in my ears, the infant in my womb leaped for joy. And blessed art thou that hast believed, because those things shall be accomplished that were spoken to thee by the Lord." Mary answered her, and pronounced the admirable canticle (Magnificat)—an eternal monument of her humility and gratitude; "A canticle more replete," says an ancient writer, "*with mysteries than words; a* glorious picture of Providence, which raises up the humble, casts down the proud, and confounds the powerful, in order to protect the weak, and satisfy the indigent:"

My soul doth magnify the Lord.

And my spirit hath rejoiced in God my Savior.

For he hath regarded the humility of his handmaid : for behold from henceforth all generations shall call me blessed.

For he that is mighty hath done great things unto me, and holy is his name.

And his mercy is from generation to generation unto them that fear him

He hath showed strength with his arm ; he hath scattered the proud in the imagination of their hearts.

He hath put down the mighty from their seats : and hath exalted the humble.

He hath filled the hungry with good things : and the rich he hath sent empty away.

He hath upholden his servant Israel : being mindful of his mercy.

As he spake unto our fathers: to Abraham and his seed for ever.

After staying three months with her

venerable cousin, Mary returned to Nazareth. At that moment, Joseph, who was a just man full of charity and veneration for the virtues of Mary, felt himself a prey to cruel perplexities. He therefore resolved to dismiss Mary. Whilst this thought occupied him, the angel of the Lord appeared to him in his sleep, and said to him, "Joseph, son of David, fear not to take unto thee Mary thy wife, for that which is conceived in her is of the Holy Ghost. And she shall bring forth a son: and thou shalt call his name Jesus. For he shall save his people from their sins." On awaking from his sleep, Joseph profoundly adored the admirable ways of Providence, and all his doubts were dissipated.

And now the solemn moment when the heavens were to rain down the Just One had arrived. Oh, mountain of Sion, leap with joy! A Virgin Mother, a Virgin excelling all the daughters of men in blessedness, is about to give to the world the Expected of the Nations!

An edict of Augustus Cæsar, then master of the world, ordered a general census of the inhabitants of the earth. Every one was obliged to go to the town from which his family sprung, to be enrolled; wherefore these holy spouses, who descended from David, notwithstanding the inclemency of the season, and the Blessed Virgin's tender condition, set out for Nazareth, and after a journey of five days, at length reached Bethlehem.

The inns were full; they sought shelter, but they found it not. The fatigue of the young virgin could not inspire compassion. Night fell; the spouses quitted the inhospitable city, sought refuge in a deserted cavern—a place which was frequented by the shepherds of Bethlehem in the stormy nights. There they rested, thanking heaven for this comfortless asylum; and there it was, in the silence of the midnight, that the Virgin brought forth the Christ expected for forty centuries, the Messiah, the Son of God, in all things equal to God, who deigned to come down into our valley of tears to renew the face of the earth, to heal and to restore; and this King of kings, this Divine Legislator, this Lord of the world, this Pastor promised to the children of Israel, now reposes on humid straw in a miserable manger. "Ah!" exclaims St. Bernard, "Ah! Mary, carefully conceal the splendor of this new Sun, lay him in the manger, cover him with his scanty clothing; that poor clothing is our wealth, the rude clothing of my Savior is more precious than purple and the manger is more glorious than the thrones of kings." Oh! what must have been Mary's joy at that moment! Let us hear St. Basil: "How shall I call thee?" exclaims the daughter of the Patriarchs, while she bends over the infant God. A mortal?—but thou hast been conceived by a Divine operation. A God?—but thou hast a human body! Ought I come to thee with incense, or offer thee my milk?—ought I bestow on thee a mother's cares, or, with forehead bowed to the dust, serve thee as thy slave?"

"And there were in the same country shepherds watching, and keeping the night-watches over their flock. And behold, an angel of the Lord stood by them, and the brightness of God shone round about them, and they feared with a great fear. And the angel said to them: Fear not; for behold I bring you good tidings of great joy, that shall be to all the people: For this day is born to you a Savior, who is Christ the Lord, in the city of David. ʽ And this shall be a sign unto you: You shall find the infant wrapped in swaddling clothes, and laid in a manger. And suddenly there was with the angel a multitude of the heavenly army, praising God, and saying: Glory to God in the highest; and on earth peace to men of good will."—Luke, ii. 8–14.

The angels retired, the celestial psalmody ceased, and the enraptured shepherds listened, till they heard only the night winds sweeping through the valley. They then took counsel of each other and said —" Let us go over to Bethlehem and see this word that is come to pass, which the Lord hath showed to us". And they came with haste; and they found Mary and Joseph, and the infant lying in the manger. And seeing, they understood of the word that had been spoken to them concerning this. And all that heard wondered: and at those things that were told them by the shepherds. But Mary kept all these words, pondering them in her heart. And the shepherds returned, glorifying and praising God for all the things they had heard and seen, as it was told unto them."—St. Luke, ii. 15-20.

Thus, for his first temple, under heaven, the Man-God had a stable.... It was there that he was circumcised, the eighth day after his nativity. As he should receive a name then, he was called Jesus, which signifies Savior; for he came to save all men.

It was in the stable that our poor God received the adoration of the shepherds of Judea, the first representatives of Israel; it was also in a stable that God, who came to save mankind, received the adoration of the princes of the East, the royal first fruits of converted Heathenism.

Forty days after this marvellous nativity of the Savior of mankind, the humle Virgin conceals the splendor of her spotless purity and the divine privilege of her virginal maternity under the sombre veils a humiliating ceremony prescribed by the law of Moses, and obligatory on every woman who had brought forth a child.

Although always a virgin, the chaste spouse of the Holy Ghost goes, as it were, to cleanse her from a stain which she had never contracted, and to join the other women of Israel in the legal purification. She presents the infant God in the Temple of Jerusalem, and likewise the two doves that should be offered in sacrifice. Here the future was unveiled to her eyes, to the eyes of her whom all nations shall call blessed, but whom all nations shall style Queen of Martyrs. Magnificent and brilliant words, it is true, fell from the prophetic lips of the aged Simeon: the child of Mary was to be a light to the nations and the glory of Israel; but he was also to be a mark for the perversity of man, and the soul of his mother was to be *transpierced by the sword of sorrow.*

Mary was saddened by these words, but she gladly accepted everything that came from God.

After this ceremony the two spouses returned to Nazareth; but they have scarcely arrived when an angel from heaven orders Joseph to take the child and his mother and fly into Egypt, for Herod sought the child to slay him.

The Wise Men who came from the East and sought the child, awakened

LIFE OF THE BLESSED VIRGIN MARY.

Herod's alarm. Herod thought that in a little while one far more potent than himself, would come to deprive him of his throne; he therefore determined to murder the child in his cradle; and to be assured of his victim, he massacred all the children of Bethlehem from two years old and under. But God will save the infant from the sword of the tyrant, and he shall live to offer himself a sacrifice on Calvary.

The angel's words terrified the hearts of Joseph and Mary: they fly by night, and pass into Egypt over roads unknown to them, and over deserts, in the midst of a thousand privations; but with them they have Jesus, and this treasure consoles them in all their sorrows, and for love of Jesus they resignedly endure all the afflictions of exile, despised as poor foreigners, by the haughty unbelievers of the land. About seven years afterwards, Herod being dead, Joseph, having received another admonition from the angel, brought back the mother and infant out of the land of exile.

The humble carpenter applied himself to his trade, the Virgin employed herself with her household duties, and Jesus, though still young, worked with his hands and assisted his poor foster father. This life of labor and meditation, this life which was so toilsome, and at the same time so interior and so perfect, this mysterious existence of Jesus, Mary, and Joseph under the humble roof of Nazareth, has remained hidden from the eyes of man.

All we know of it is, that when the Divine infant had attained his twelfth year, Mary and Joseph, who were strict observers of the Mosaic law, brought him to Jerusalem for the feast of the Pasch. Here they lost him, and thinking that he was with some of their kindred or acquaintances, they were returning from the holy city, when they discovered their mistake. Extreme was their desolation: they hastened back, they sought him in all the streets of the city, and after lengthened inquiries found him in the Temple, seated in the midst of the doctors, astonishing them by his wisdom and answers. "Son, why hast thou done so to us?" asked his mother tenderly; "behold thy father and I have sought thee sorrowing." Jesus answered: "How is is that ye sought me? did you not know that I must be about my Father's business?" But they did not comprehend what he said. He then accompanied them, and remained at Nazareth subject to them. And his mother kept all these words in her heart, and Jesus advanced in wisdom and age and grace with God and man.

In these few words the Sacred Scriptures epitomize many years of our Savior's life. For a period of about eighteen years the Holy Family remains hidden from our eyes.

It is believed that our Lord was twenty-nine years of age when Joseph died: a most enviable death. After embracing his adopted Son, he departed this life, accompanied by the profound regrets of his loving child.

The Man-God is now about to commence his divine mission: he tears himself from the embraces of his holy Mother, quits Nazareth, and retires into the desert to prepare himself, by fasting and prayer, for the grand work of saving the world. After this Jesus dwells a short while with Mary, to calm her anguish and console the troubled heart of that tender mother by his presence.

It was then that the marriage of Cana in Galilee was solemnized. The spouses were related to the Blessed Virgin. She was invited to the wedding, together with Jesus and his first disciples. The wine failed at the banquet: the spouses were confounded. Mary was the first to perceive their confusion and embarrassment; she turned to Jesus, and full of confidence and faith she said to him: "They have no wine." And she waited till the moment when her Son's interposition should become necessary. Jesus, unable to resist the charitable desires of his mother, works his first miracle at her instance, and changes the water contained in six stone urns into delicious wine.

The better to understand some passages

of Scripture in which Jesus seems to have spoken with apparent coldness to his mother, we deem it opportune to make the following few remarks:—None can doubt the extreme and profound tenderness with which Christ reciprocated the tenderness and affection of Mary. From her he had received existence and the blood that flowed in his veins: the blood that he was to offer in sacrifice on the cross to take away the sins of the world was the gift of Mary, and of Mary alone

All the holy affections which the Lord of life implants in the soul of a child for those from whom it receives life—all those holy affections did our Lord Jesus concentrate in the person of his blessed Mother. As God and Man he loved this tender mother; of her he had taken flesh, and as God he loved her with a love transcending all that is earthly. This was the only time in which the Divinity, who conferreth all good, found himself called upon to practise towards the creature the virtue of noble hearts, gratitude; and that of Jesus for Mary augmented in proportion to all the sacrifices, privations, and labors that this holy and noble Virgin underwent for love of him. If, therefore, we occasionally find in the Scriptures, that Christ sometimes spoke to his mother more like her Lord than her Son, it is not because he lacked affection, or that he was indifferent to her, but it is simply because he isolated himself from earthly things, that he might the better glorify his Father, whose interests were his primary consideration—interests of such superlative nature as to occupy wholly the soul of the Divine Redeemer. Mary was too deeply impressed with the conviction of the sacred mission of her Son to be troubled at his words, if they sometimes seemed severe she knew that the young Galilean whom she had nourished at her breast was to become the Legislator, and she knew full well that he would soon cause the miraculous transformation to take place; in a word, she was intimately persuaded that her divine Son would not fail to perform the miracle in favor of the guests, and at her request.

The Gospel, except on two occasions, does not make further mention of Mary, till the time of our Lord's passion. The first is when a woman, enraptured by the discourses of Jesus, exclaimed, "Blessed are the breasts that gave thee suck." But Jesus immediately replied, "Blessed are those who hear the Word of God and keep it." Jesus wished thus publicly to congratulate Mary less for being his mother, than for having merited this honor by her submission to the will of God. Behold, he seems to say to them, what you should imitate in my mother! The second occasion is, when some one came to Jesus whilst he was instructing the people, and said to him that his Mother was there; Jesus replied, looking round on his disciples, "My mother and my brethren are those who hear the Word of God and keep it."

This answer which, under other circumstances, might seem stern, was perfectly mysterious, and at the same time necessary, in relation to those who were listening to him. The Jews, to whom he was announcing the kingdom of heaven, regarded him as a mere man, and were accustomed to say, "Is not this the son of Joseph the carpenter?—Is not his mother called Mary?—are not his relatives amongst us?" Our Savior, therefore, would have them regard him not as solely the son of Mary, but rather that they should recognize in his person the character of his divinity, which they would not acknowledge, although he clearly manifested it by his words and works.

It is certain that Mary followed Jesus in all his journeys, and that she accompanied the holy women of whom the Scripture makes occasional mention, giving us to understand that they attached themselves to the person of the Divine Redeemer. How could we doubt this, when we find her following her Son amidst all his ignominies, standing at the foot of the cross, and mingling her tears with the blood of her Son? And, oh! during the three last years of the life of Jesus, how much had her tender soul to suffer amidst every species of persecution and sorrows that man heaped upon her divine Son. But Mary was always filled with a holy resignation—always inspired with sentiments of entire subjection to God; nay, in the midst of all those tribulations, alarms, and insults, she proved herself to be the most perfect as well as the most admirable of mothers. "Mary," says a pious writer, "was not only a holy dove hiding herself in the crevices of the rock —a pure Virgin, chosen to feed with her milk, and cradle in her arms, a heavenly guest: she was likewise a valiant woman, whom the Lord was pleased to place in all the situations and trials of life, in order that the daughters of Eve might have an example to follow, and a model to imitate." In her hours of desolation, in the garden of Gethsemane, in the judgment hall, and on Calvary, the mother of Jesus must have remembered the words of aged Simeon, and she must have felt the sword of grief piercing her soul. Oh! how truly might not that afflicted mother have exclaimed in these moments—" All ye who pass the way, come and see if there be grief like mine." O God! at this dread hour what a sacrifice didst thou demand from the Mother and Son!

At last the grand mystery of man's salvation approaches its completion: the august victim is on the altar. Jesus, overwhelmed with afflictions, has no more blood to shed, and is about to breathe his last gasp; it is then he addressed the last words to Mary; he bequeaths his mother to the well-beloved disciple, and the well-beloved disciple to his Mother: "Woman, behold thy son," and then, "John, behold thy mother." Such was the last proof of the immense love of Jesus for men. He left them Mary for a mother; for in the person of Saint John has he not called all mankind her children? and ever since then Mary has not ceased to employ her all-powerful intercession with Jesus Christ in our behalf, and to discharge for us all, just as well as sinners, the duties of the tenderest of mothers.

When the adorable body of Jesus was taken down from the cross, his holy Mother received it in her arms, and upon her knees was laid the bleeding and mutilated form of the Man-God. But, oh! what was her joy, when she beheld her Son and her God triumphing over the grave, and when, a little while afterwards, she assisted at his glorious ascension. Beholding the splendors of heaven revealed to her eyes—beholding the ineffable glories of her Son, must not Mary have been the happiest of mothers?

The Scripture does not tell us that Jesus Christ appeared to his mother after his Resurrection; but who could doubt it? She was the last whom he named in the hour of his death; and surely, it is only reasonable to suppose that she was one of the first to whom he appeared after his Resurrection. After having accompanied him to Jerusalem with the apostles and holy women, she doubtless went with the former into Galilee, and then returned with them to Jerusalem, where, according to St. Luke, she remained from the moment of her Son's ascension till the descent of the Holy Ghost upon the apostles.

When the promised Paraclete descended on the apostles, who persevered unanimously in prayer, she too was present, thus becoming, as it were, the luminous column that guided the first steps of the new born Church.

The Holy Scriptures say nothing of the late years of Mary. It is thought that she retired for some years from Jerusalem, when the persecution broke out which (about the year 44) compelled the apostles to fly from the deicide city. It would appear that she went with her adopted son, St. John, to the city of Ephesus; and some authors are of opinion that she died there. The most commonly received opinion is, that she expired in Jerusalem, surrounded by the apostles and disciples of Jesus.

Hers was less a death than a tranquil sleep, in which the most perfect and most humble of creatures, the best-beloved daughter of the Heavenly Father, the chaste spouse of the Holy Ghost, the devout Mother of the Son, quitted her long exile, to go and take her seat on a hrone at the right hand of Jesus, eminently raised above all the elect and angels.

It is commonly believed that Mary died on the night of the 15th of August, in the forty-sixth year of our era. Others think that her death occurred in the fifth year of the reign of Claudius, *i. e.*, in the 798th year of Rome, or forty-fifth of the Christian era. Some say that she lived sixty-one years, others fifty-two, and others sixty-two; whilst some believe that she passed seventy-two years here below.

Whilst Jesus Christ was crowning his blessed Mother in heaven, constituting her queen of heaven and earth, the mourning apostles entombed her virginal body in Gethsemane.

Three days after her august obsequies, Thomas, who alone was absent at the time of her decease, returned from a distant region. He wished once more to contemplate the features of the Mother of Jesus, to gaze once more on the living ark of the Most High, on the tabernacle of the Word made Flesh. Thereon the sepulchre was opened; but according to St. John of Damascus, and the greater number of the Greek and Latin Fathers, the sacred body was not to be found. It had gone to be reunited to its holy soul, and to enjoy never-ending happiness. The most pure and immaculate body of the Virgin was not to be a prey to the corruption of the sepulchre; and according to the expression of the hymn sung on the Feast of the Assumption, *"Death was not to hold in its chains her who had given to the world the Author of life."*

PRAYER.

O Virgin, abyss of perfections, imperishable treasure of graces! O Mary, our all-powerful Mother, thou hope of Christians, queen of angels and of the world! deign to watch over us on the perilous ways of our sad pilgrimage, and grant, we beseech thee, that we may be made partakers of the blessedness that thou art now enjoying in heaven. *Amen.*

THE LITANY OF THE BLESSED VIRGIN.

Anthem.

We fly to thy patronage, O holy Mother of God! despise not our prayers in our necessities, but deliver us from all dangers, O thou ever glorious and blessed Virgin!

Lord, have mercy on us.

Christ, have mercy on us.

Lord, have mercy on us.
Christ, hear us.
Christ, graciously hear us.
God, the Father of Heaven, *have mercy on us.*
God, the Son, Redeemer of the world, *have mercy on us.*
God, the Holy Ghost, *have mercy on us.*
Holy Trinity, one God, *have mercy on us.*
Holy Mary,
Holy Mother of God,
Holy Virgin of virgins,
Mother of Christ,
Mother of divine grace,
Most pure mother,
Most chaste mother,
Mother undefiled,
Mother inviolate,
Most amiable mother,
Most admirable mother,
Mother of our Creator,

Pray for us.

Mother of our Redeemer,
Most prudent virgin,
Most venerable virgin,
Most renowned virgin,
Most powerful virgin,
Most merciful virgin,
Most faithful virgin,
Mirror of justice,
Seat of wisdom,
Cause of our joy,
Spiritual vessel,
Honorable vessel,
Vessel of singular devotion,
Mystical rose,
Tower of David,
Tower of ivory,
House of gold,
Ark of the covenant,
Gate of Heaven,
Morning star,
Health of the weak,

Pray for us.

LIFE OF THE BLESSED VIRGIN MARY.

Refuge of sinners,
Comforter of the afflicted,
Help of Christians,
Queen of angels,
Queen of patriarchs,
Queen of prophets,
Queen of apostles,
Queen of martyrs,
Queen of confessors,
Queen of virgins,
Queen of all saints,
Holy Mary, conceived without original sin,

Pray for us.

Lamb of God, who takest away the sins of the world, *Spare us, O Lord!*

Lamb of God, who takest away the inss of the world, *Graciously hear us, O Lord!*

Lamb of God, who takest away the sins of the world, *Have mercy on us, O Lord!*

Christ, hear us. Christ, graciously

hear us. Lord, have mercy on us. Christ, have mercy on us. Lord, have mercy on us.

Our Father, &c.

V. Pray for us, O holy Mother of God!

R. That we may be made worthy of the promises of Christ.

PRAYER.

Pour forth, we beseech thee, O Lord! thy grace into our hearts, that we, to whom the incarnation of Christ, thy Son, was made known by the message of an angel, may, by his passion and cross, be brought to the glory of his resurrection through the same Jesus Christ our Lord. Amen.

THE CONSOLING THOUGHTS

OF

ST. FRANCIS DE SALES.

The writings of St. Francis de Sales are the fruit of grace and experience. — *Fenelon.*

In his writings we have the morality of the Sacred Scriptures and the Holy Fathers reduced to true principles and practical rules. — *Père de Tournemine.*

Francis de Sales is truly sublime: there is no one among moderns with such sweetness, who has a hand so steady and experienced as his, to elevate souls to perfection and to detach them from themselves. — *Bossuet.*

The doctrine of St. Francis de Sales is a food, not of earth but of heaven, which, from the same substance, nourishes, like the manna, all kinds of persons; and I am able to say, without offending against the respect which I owe to all other writers, that after the Holy Scriptures there are no works that have better maintained piety among the faithful than those of this holy bishop. — *Bourdaloue.*

I conjure you anew to make the works of M. de Sales your delight and your dearest study. I have read them I cannot tell how many times, and I would not dispense myself from reading them again : they never lose the charm of novelty : they always seem to me to say something more than they had said before. Such is my opinion of this great Saint. — *Pope Alexander VII.*

You cannot read anything more useful than the works of St. Francis de Sales in which everything is pleasing and consoling. — *Fenelon.*

The very title of the book pleases, and should secure a large number of readers. How many souls are there to-day who stand in need of being encouraged and consoled? . . . . Blessed, then, be the pious author who has received the happy inspiration of assembling together the CONSOLING THOUGHTS OF ST. FRANCIS DE SALES, the sweetest and most amiable of the Saints and one of the greatest masters of the spiritual life. — *Catholic Bibliography.*

Bound in Cloth Extra, Red Burnished Edges.

Price, $1.00.

O'LOUGHLIN & McLAUGHLIN,

630 Washington St., Boston, Mass.

www.ingramcontent.com/pod-product-compliance
Lightning Source LLC
Chambersburg PA
CBHW020158170426
43199CB00010B/1098